THIS BOOK
IS FOR
THE BIRDS

and
for YOU
my ZiGGY FRiEND!

More Big Laughs from SIGNET

THIS BOOK IS FOR THE BIRDS

by Tom Wilson

A SIGNET BOOK

NEW AMERICAN LIBRARY

TIMES MIRROR

8

11

16

17

18

20

THE BIRDS SING FOR SOME PEOPLE..

...i JUST SPOTTED THE
FIRST SPRING ROBIN...

...THE FIRST SPRING
ROBIN JUST SPOTTED
ME !!

YEAH...HE'S HERE AT THE PET SHOP, ZIGGY ...SAYS HE DOESN'T LIKE YOUR CHOICE OF TV SHOWS...HIS CAGE IS DRAFTY, AND YOU'RE A LOUSY CONVERSATIONALIST

41

42

FRIENDS ARE PEOPLE
YOU LIKE,
...WHO LIKE YOU
RIGHT BACK !!

...LOOKS LIKE
IT'S GONNA BE
ONE OF THOSE
KINDA DAYS !!